PATIENT A

BY LEE BLESSING

★

DRAMATISTS
PLAY SERVICE
INC.

PATIENT A
Copyright © 1993, Lee Blessing

All Rights Reserved

CAUTION: Professionals and amateurs are hereby warned that performance of PATIENT A is subject to payment of a royalty. It is fully protected under the copyright laws of the United States of America, and of all countries covered by the International Copyright Union (including the Dominion of Canada and the rest of the British Commonwealth), and of all countries covered by the Pan-American Copyright Convention, the Universal Copyright Convention, the Berne Convention, and of all countries with which the United States has reciprocal copyright relations. All rights, including without limitation professional/amateur stage rights, motion picture, recitation, lecturing, public reading, radio broadcasting, television, video or sound recording, all other forms of mechanical, electronic and digital reproduction, transmission and distribution, such as CD, DVD, the Internet, private and file-sharing networks, information storage and retrieval systems, photocopying, and the rights of translation into foreign languages are strictly reserved. Particular emphasis is placed upon the matter of readings, permission for which must be secured from the Author's agent in writing.

The English language stock and amateur stage performance rights in the United States, its territories, possessions and Canada for PATIENT A are controlled exclusively by DRAMATISTS PLAY SERVICE, INC., 440 Park Avenue South, New York, NY 10016. No professional or nonprofessional performance of the Play may be given without obtaining in advance the written permission of DRAMATISTS PLAY SERVICE, INC., and paying the requisite fee.

Inquiries concerning all other rights should be addressed to Judy Boals, Inc., 307 West 38th Street, #812, New York, NY 10018. Attn: Judy Boals.

SPECIAL NOTE

Anyone receiving permission to produce PATIENT A is required to give credit to the Author as sole and exclusive Author of the Play on the title page of all programs distributed in connection with performances of the Play and in all instances in which the title of the Play appears for purposes of advertising, publicizing or otherwise exploiting the Play and/or a production thereof. The name of the Author must appear on a separate line, in which no other name appears, immediately beneath the title and in size of type equal to 50% of the size of the largest, most prominent letter used for the title of the Play. No person, firm or entity may receive credit larger or more prominent than that accorded the Author. The following acknowledgment must appear on the title page in all programs distributed in connection with performances of the Play:

Originally Produced by Signature Theatre Company,
James Houghton, Artistic Director,
Thomas C. Proehl, Managing Director.

To Jeanne,
for every step of the way

We are all special cases. We all want to appeal against something! Everyone insists on his innocence, at all costs, even if it means accusing the rest of the human race and heaven.

— Camus, *La Chute*

Assuredly we bring not innocence into the world, we bring impurity much rather: that which purifies us is trial, and trial is by what is contrary.

— Milton, *Areopagitica*

PATIENT A was first produced at Signature Theatre Company (James Houghton, Artistic Director; Thomas C. Proehl, Managing Director), in New York City, on April 23, 1993. It was directed by Jeanne Blake; the costume design was by Teresa Snider-Stein; the lighting design was by Jeffrey S. Koger and the production stage manager was Kurt Engstrom. The cast was as follows:

KIMBERLY	Robin Morse
LEE	Jon DeVries
MATTHEW	Richard Bekins

CHARACTERS

(in alphabetical order)

KIM, in her early twenties
LEE, in his forties
MATTHEW, about thirty

PATIENT A

Lights up to reveal Matthew, sitting upstage. He very slowly pages through an invisible magazine. Kim enters. She looks around as though this is the first time she's ever been here. She notices Matthew, who gives her a small, friendly wave and goes back to his magazine. Kim sits downstage on a platform. Lee enters. He makes a gesture for Kim to lie down on the platform, parallel to the audience line. She does so, and closes her eyes. Lee looks down at her.

LEE. *(Reciting in a natural tone.)*
"The wanton troopers riding by
Have shot my fawn, and it will die.
Ungentle men! They cannot thrive
To kill thee. Thou ne'er didst alive
Them any harm: alas, nor could
Thy death yet do them any good.
I'm sure I never wished them ill;
Nor do I for all this; nor will."

(To audience.)
I heard somewhere, years ago, stumbling forward or backward — I can't remember which — in my career, that if you have an actor lie feet-first to the audience, then it's a tragedy. But if you have her lie head-first —
KIM. Should I do that?
LEE. No, no. If you have her lie head-first, then it's a comedy. *(Staring at her a moment.)* Or it's the other way around. I can't remember. It was a director talking. Anyway, the position itself preconditions us.
KIM. But you've got me lying sideways. *(Sitting up.)* That's

not anything, right? I mean, not tragedy or comedy.
LEE. Well —
KIM. Why? I'm not neutral.
LEE. I know — I know you're not. But I am. *(She gives him a look, then indicates Matthew.)*
KIM. Who's he?
LEE. Him? Oh, that's ... I thought he might be helpful later.
KIM. I trust you, you know.
LEE. I know. *(A beat.)*
KIM. What was that poem, anyway?
LEE. What?
KIM. The poem you were saying.
LEE. Oh — actually, that's one of my favorite poems.
KIM. It is?
LEE. It's not very current. Andrew Marvell. The "Coy Mistress" guy? *(She's unsure.)* Doesn't matter.
KIM. Was that the whole poem?
LEE. No, no. Only the beginning. It's actually a hundred and twenty-two lines long. Short lines. It's called, "The Nymph Complaining For The Death Of Her Fawn." Mid-1600s. It's in the voice of the nymph — or young girl. It's really about the loss of innocence. The convention however is that it's about the death of ... of a pet.
KIM. A pet?
LEE. A pet fawn. *(A beat.)*
KIM. I'm a little stumped by this.
LEE. I'm sorry. It's kind of personal for me. I'm trying to find a ... a resonance. Something that's evocative for me. Of you. Of your story.
KIM. I had a lot of pets.
LEE. It's not that literal.
KIM. Birds, a dog — no small deer.
LEE. It's more figurative than that.
KIM. Why do you have to be figurative? Why don't you just tell my story?
MATTHEW. He's a playwright.

KIM.   *(Looking at Matthew, then to Lee.)* Ok, who are the troopers?
LEE.   The troop — ? Oh, um ... "The wanton troopers riding by" — yes. That's actually a reference to the Scottish Covenanting Army which invaded England in 1640 —
KIM.   Stop.
LEE.   Yes?
KIM.   What have they got to do with me?
LEE.   Nothing ... directly. But they were raiders, lived off the land and ... killed a fawn. Or men like them did. It's all fiction anyway. The poem just needs the fawn to be killed by people who don't really ... take responsibility.
KIM.   Oh! Ok. Go on.
LEE.   Really?

" ... But, O my fears!
It cannot die so. Heaven's King
Keeps register of everything:
And nothing may we use in vain.
E'en beasts must be with justice slain,
Else men are made their deodands."

MATTHEW.   Deodands? *(They stare at Matthew.)*
LEE.   Legal term. Means forfeits. Not important.
KIM.   This is very personal for you, isn't it?
LEE.   Yes, I guess it is.
KIM.   'Cause it makes no sense to me at all. I was trained to be an actuary. You know? Working out mortality rates —
LEE.   This was a mortality.
KIM.   A *fawn?*
LEE.   You were a mortality.
KIM.   I'm going to do this my own way for a while. Ok? Just to get started. *(He nods. She makes a small gesture. He sits. She speaks to the audience.)* For those of you who don't know who I am yet — and it's already several minutes into the play and I'm sure that's some kind of playwriting mistake — my name is ... was ... Kimberly Ann Mary Bergalis. I came from a fam-

ily of Lithuanian-American Catholics, for the most part. I'm using the past tense, by the way, out of respect for myself. The rest of my family's doing fine.

LEE. Past tense is a very workable choice.

KIM. *(To audience, giving him a look.)* I was born in eastern Pennsylvania, and grew up in a little town called Tamaqua. Lee actually came there for my funeral.

LEE. I was struck by — May I interrupt?

KIM. Is it poetry?

LEE. No.

KIM. Ok.

LEE. *(To audience.)* I was struck by the countryside. There are ridges everywhere you look. They loom over you. Towns in dark, narrow valleys. Buildings, roads, mines — all of it with this eternally leftover look. Even the fast-food places feel like they were built a hundred years ago.

MATTHEW. He thought —

LEE. Who would want to be buried here?

KIM. But he hadn't seen the cemetary. On top of the ridge, up among the trees. As far as you look, other trees, other ridges. And the sky — you're practically in the sky. It's a Lithuanian cemetary. Names like —

MATTHEW. Karalunas, Andrukitis, Shucavage, Pilashusky. And of course, Zebleckas —

KIM. My grandmother. *(Quickly, to Lee.)* Is this how he's going to be helpful?

LEE. Maybe.

KIM. *(To audience.)* Anyway, my grandmother was buried there, and I wanted to be buried next to her. And now I am, of course. I believe in an afterlife, and I'm with her now. In heaven.

LEE. Let's not get too much into that.

KIM. Why not?

LEE. It just makes me a little uncomfortable. Concepts like a literal heaven.

KIM. You don't believe in one?

LEE. I have no faith.

KIM. Really? So what's heaven for you? Things in the world?

LEE. Yes, I guess.
KIM. Like the poem?
LEE. Maybe.
KIM. So heaven for you comes in little bits and pieces?
LEE. Yes.
KIM. And ends. Finally.
LEE. Yes.
KIM. I see. *(To audience.)* When I was twelve, we moved to Ft. Pierce, Florida. I loved it. I was just beginning junior-high, and suddenly it was summer forever. I found a best friend almost right away — Geralynn. We were blood sisters. That got looked into later on. Sometimes when we didn't have anything else to do, we'd take a stupid little red plastic boat and go float in the Indian River.
LEE. *(To audience.)* Geralynn told me about this. The image stuck in my head.
MATTHEW. *(Without looking up.)* It did?
KIM. Geri and I would float in that boat in the sun for hours. Like we were the same organism. I don't know which gave me the most pleasure — the floating itself or being that close to another person. The river's not deep there, but I used to imagine that it went down forever, like the sea. That we were above a world that had no limit, just floating. *(A beat.)* My Dad was the financial director for the city of Ft. Pierce. His name is George.
LEE. *(To audience.)* A lot of daughters love and admire their fathers. Kim emulated hers. She sought his respect in everything.
MATTHEW. Sort of a perfect relationship?
LEE. A fortunate one.
KIM. My mother, Anna, in the first of a series of ironies the author wants me to observe — although I find them pretty unremarkable — was a nurse at a clinic that treated a lot of AIDS patients. *(A beat.)* After high-school I went to the University of Florida. I was a business major, and — *(Lee coughs quietly.)* Oh. He wants me to underscore this other irony. You know, that I was going to be an actuary, and that actuaries work a lot with statistics, and that eventually that's what I be-

came — a statistic, not an actuary. Ok?
LEE. Thanks.
KIM. I'm not sure these are technically even ironies.
MATTHEW. Besides, didn't they do this on Channel 5?
LEE. Humor me.
KIM. The other irony — and believe me, this is the last one — is that when I was in high school I once tried to do a report on AIDS, but had to pick another subject, because there wasn't enough material on it in the library. Are ironies like poems for you or something?
LEE. A little.
KIM. So you actually get pleasure from them? 'Cause most people don't, you know. *(To audience.)* In the middle of my junior year, I needed some dental work. Two back molars had to come out. *(A beat.)* We'd just changed our dentist. Our new one was down in Jensen — Dr. Acer.*
LEE. Dr. Acer.
KIM. What?
LEE. Oh, nothing. Dr. Acer, that's all. I've been thinking what to do with him.
MATTHEW. What to do?
LEE. All I can see is that terrible graduation shot of him that ran all over the country. *(To audience.)* Grainy, black-and-white.... The very quality of the shot — the remoteness it forced on you.... It made him look like a criminal.
MATTHEW. A criminal?
LEE. I'm not saying he was. There could've been accidents, oversights. Certainly no one ever proved that he willfully infected anyone. He even published a letter, the day before he died. It said he had HIV. It also said he'd been advised he could continue to practice, as long as he followed the guidelines of the Centers for Disease Control. If any of his patients was worried however, they should get tested. The last paragraph was quite touching.
MATTHEW. *(Quoting it.)* "Please try to understand. I am a

---

* Pronounced, "Ack-er."

gentle man. To infect anyone would be contrary to everything I have stood for."

LEE. As it turned out, he'd infected at least six of his patients with HIV. The questions these events raised were all ugly ones: had Dr. Acer deliberately transmitted the virus? Had he done it negligently? Or — even more disturbing — was he trying to follow the CDC's guidelines? No one knew the answers to these questions. And Dr. Acer was dead. All that was left was a blood sample and a tiny, black-and-white photo. *(A beat.)* This is all we have to judge by, so many of us. On one hand we see a young, composed, telegenic woman dying. On the other, this little grey, remote head. This dead man. This mysterious letter in a newspaper.

MATTHEW. And you think that's fair?

LEE. Some stories just push us in a particular direction. We have to face that, we have to give it its due in a sense — and yet struggle to withhold our final judgment.

MATTHEW. And who are you to judge?

KIM. Yes, who are you?

LEE. Nobody.

KIM. *(To audience.)* On December 17, 1987 I had two back molars removed by Dr. Acer. While it was an involved appointment, I don't remember much about it that was unusual. Of course, it was years before it seemed important enough to remember. I drove home on the narrow road up the coast, looking at the ocean and the trees. *(A beat.)* Less than four years later, I'd be dead.

LEE.
"Though they should wash their guilty hands
In this warm life-blood, which doth part
From thine, and wound me to the heart,
Yet could they not be clean: their stain
Is dyed in such a purple grain,
There is not such another in
The world, to offer for their sin."

MATTHEW. That's a little extreme, isn't it?

LEE. What? Oh — hyperbole is a central device of the poem. The fawn is seen as a perfect ideal of innocence. To

harm it was a profound sin. I'm not saying that's Kim's story exactly.
MATTHEW. Then what are you saying?
LEE. That I miss ... innocence.
KIM. *(To the audience.)* I started to feel sick in spring of 1989 — only about a year and a half after I had my molars removed. Part of the reason we didn't at first think of Dr. Acer was that it had been so recent. But I was definitely getting sick. I had a few sore throats that spring, and then I developed oral thrush. Little white patches in my mouth. The doctor was surprised. Normally they only see thrush in diabetics or people on a lot of antibiotics, infants, AIDS patients. They gave me some medication and it cleared up. A few weeks later though, the thrush came back. Meanwhile, we looked for diabetes. My grandfather was diabetic.
MATTHEW. A basic medical principle: look for the likeliest first.
KIM. I had a blood sugar test done. Everything was fine. Then I started fainting at work. I went to a hemotologist. They took blood, ran a lot of tests — no HIV test, though. I really didn't fit the profile.
MATTHEW. Look for the likeliest first.
KIM. The blood results weren't good. I began to have problems breathing. I went to a hemotologist/oncologist, who examined me for cancer.
MATTHEW. Look for the likeliest —
KIM. *I know.* I drove home to show my parents all the lab information. My Mom cried. She said my symptoms were so reminiscent of AIDS.
MATTHEW. Did you have a test done —
LEE. She asked —
KIM. No, I said. There's no reason. *(A beat.)* I just got worse. I didn't have cancer. The doctors wondered if I was just hyperventilating. By December my parents had to come up and drive me home. Just before we left, a nurse called and said the new results had come in and that I had hepatitis. Hepatitis, I thought. That's lucky.
LEE. When I grew up, it was the diseases that were dying.

Smallpox, polio, diphtheria — wonderful new drugs were killing off all the old killers. Billions of tiny white flags under the microscopes — that was the image. I think the public genuinely believed we could defeat any serious, infectious disease.
KIM. Except for viruses.
LEE. Except for viruses. They've been with us forever, presumably, though we didn't discover the first human virus until 1900.
MATTHEW. Yellow fever. *(To Lee.)* Do I really have to do this?
LEE. What do you mean?
MATTHEW. This choral support. I mean, can't we just talk?
LEE. We are talking.
MATTHEW. No — to each other.
LEE. This is important information.
MATTHEW. But it's yours, not mine. I didn't even exist in the decade you're talking about. For that matter, do I exist now?
KIM. What's it matter?
MATTHEW. What's it *matter?*
KIM. *(To Lee.)* Who is he?
LEE. Can we just talk about viruses? We do not have all night.
MATTHEW. I like her question. Who am I?
LEE. *(To audience.)* Viruses infect every living thing. And while the vast majority don't kill their host —
MATTHEW. Who am I?
LEE. Which would be inefficient —
MATTHEW. Do I have a name?
LEE. Some do. *(To Matthew.)* Will you please shut up?! *(Matthew stares at him. Lee continues quietly to the audience.)* It doesn't always last. The great influenza pandemic of 1918 came, killed millions and left. Some viruses hover around us forever, like rabies. *(To Matthew.)* I'm sorry. *(A beat.)* I'm sorry. Please forgive me.
MATTHEW. Who am I to forgive? *(A beat.)*
LEE. *(To Kim.)* Meanwhile, you thought you had hepatitis.
KIM. *(To audience.)* By the time my folks got me home, I

could barely walk. I blacked out and crashed into the hall closet. The next day we got a call from the doctor's office. I didn't have hepatitis. It was a mistake in their labs.

MATTHEW. A basic medical principle: sometimes we make mistakes.

KIM. Our local doctor diagnosed me with bilateral pneumocystis pneumonia and had me hospitalized. Oh, yes — and for the first time I was tested for HIV. The test wasn't conclusive. So I had another one. That was inconclusive too. So I had one more. Five days after I turned twenty-two, the results came back positive.

LEE. What with the pneumocystis and the numbers, it was clear they were talking about AIDS.

KIM. The doctor gave me some time alone, before my folks came in. I began to cry. I looked out the window, and the clouds were moving against the sun, swirling. My life came into my mind. I thought about when I lived in Tamaqua, and the lake and ice skating, and then when I became, you know, a woman. I thought of everything, and that it was all over. No boyfriend, husband, kids, grandkids. My eyes were closed. Suddenly I felt as if someone was lying by my side. There was pressure against my whole side, a warmth — I felt it. I heard a voice that said it would all be ok. That everyone in the family would be able to handle it. And I opened my eyes and no one was in the room.

LEE. Kim was an adult of course, so the law said that only she could tell her parents.

KIM. My mother was the first to come in. She knew as soon as she looked at me. She came around and just lunged onto the bed and cried and hugged me and pushed my hair back, and ... comforted me. She talked about her own parents, who'd been killed years before in a car accident and how they'd be waiting in heaven for me, along with Grandma Zebleckas and even their dog that died, too. I think if she could have put everything that ever lived into heaven for me in that moment she would have.

MATTHEW. *(To Lee.)* Millions go through this.

LEE. And will.

KIM. When we'd calmed down, my father came in. That was harder. I was his oldest. I remember he said —
MATTHEW. *(Softly, as the father.)* "Oh, my God, no. No, please."
KIM. And he shook, and he cried. I said "Put your head on my shoulder," and he did. And I ... petted his head, and said, "It's gonna be ok. We're gonna get through this." And Mom was rubbing his back, and he just kept crying and crying. He kept saying it had to be a mistake, that he didn't believe it, that it can't be. It just can't be. And I said, "Dad, it is."
LEE. *(To audience.)* Kim's mother went to work the next day, trying to keep her mind off it. But the day after was Saturday, and there was nothing to do but think. *(Lee looks expectantly at Matthew, who's lost in thought.)* She had nothing to do but think. *(Matthew looks up.)*
MATTHEW. Oh. *(To audience.)* It was a cold, wet, foggy day, but she had to get out of the house. So she went for a walk on the beach. Almost purposely she headed for an isolated area where some women had been attacked. She decided to look for a large piece of driftwood — a big club, she thought — and to beat the hell out of anyone who tried to hurt her. There was only one person on the beach, a retired man surfcasting. A few yards behind him there was a broken branch in the sand. Anna picked it up and glanced at the man, who said —
LEE. Lady, I'm just here fishing.
KIM. I'm going for a walk. I found out my daughter's very sick.
LEE. Oh.
MATTHEW. Then she strode down the beach, looking for someone guilty. She didn't find anyone. Then she came back.
LEE. Looks like you cooled down a little. Want to talk about it?
KIM. Not now.
MATTHEW. She dropped the piece of wood and kept walking. When she was almost out of earshot he yelled —
LEE. Lady! Life is unfair!
MATTHEW. She didn't turn. She just walked home.

LEE. *(After a beat, to audience.)*
"It is a wondrous thing, how fleet
'Twas, on those little silver feet.
With what a pretty skipping grace,
It oft would challenge me the race:
And when't had left me far away,
'Twould stay, and run again, and stay."

(To audience.) "It," by the way, refers to the fawn — or innocence — or I suppose, for me anyway, just life.

"For it was nimbler much than hinds;
And trod, as on the four winds."

(To audience.) I didn't meet Kim till the last months of her life. She was in the hospital, she'd just had a transfusion. I'm really pretty useless in hospitals. *(A beat.)* A few years ago a friend of mine died. Congenital heart defect. She'd had surgery when she was young, and that gave her maybe twenty more years — but suddenly one day the sutures or plugs blew, and.... So for the first time in my life, I went to an intensive care ward, to see Serene, which was her name. It was so *hot* in there. All this equipment, all these beds and noise ... I tried to smile, talk normally. She couldn't talk at all — she had these tubes and things going into her throat. I'd never seen the life in a person so ... pressed down into her. My reaction was absolutely physical. I started to faint. Just from being near this terrible force that was working in her. I stumbled out into the waiting room, collapsed in the nearest chair. I felt as though I'd been sealed in my own crypt.
KIM. I saw that all the time. People who visited me, journalists, friends. Some couldn't take it.
LEE. When I first met you, I couldn't touch you.
KIM. I know. I was used to that, too.
LEE. I knew it was safe. I know it's safe.
KIM. Just makes you human.
LEE. It makes me common. I can take my place in the clear majority. *(A beat.)*

KIM. Maybe if I just went on with my story.

LEE. We could try that.

KIM. *(To audience.)* My case was reported to the state agency and also to the Centers For Disease Control in Atlanta. They couldn't figure out how I'd been infected. I didn't have any of the usual risk factors. I hadn't had any transfusions. I wasn't a drug user or hemophiliac. They ended up asking about some pretty unusual things.

MATTHEW. What about this blood sister you're supposed to have had? This Geralynn — ?

KIM. Yes?

MATTHEW. When was that?

KIM. Eighth or ninth grade.

MATTHEW. And how did you, um — ?

KIM. We took a pin and just, you know, pricked our fingers, rubbed our fingers together — and we came up with some contract that we were sisters forever and put the fingerprint by the names. We used a little safety pin. There was just a tiny dot.

MATTHEW. How many people have you had intercourse with?

KIM. None.

MATTHEW. I'm talking about sex, now. Sexual —

KIM. None. *(To audience.)* They had a very hard time believing that I'd never had intercourse. They came back and asked the questions again. And they made them more personal.

MATTHEW. Have you ever used any birth control devices or pills?

KIM. No.

MATTHEW. Did any of your boyfriends ever use birth control devices?

KIM. Once, in my junior year in college. But nothing came of it.

MATTHEW. And what were the circumstances of his using it?

KIM. He had ... placed the condom, and we were, you know, talking about it, and we were going to. And my roommate at the time had moved out two weeks earlier. Anyway,

there was a slamming, and he thought she had come in, and my bedroom door was open. And he jumped up, and I said "No — it's not my roommate, it's someone across the hall." And he apologized and.... So nothing ever came of it. We both just went to sleep.
MATTHEW. So you never — ?
KIM. No.
MATTHEW. Have you ever participated in oral sex?
KIM. *(To audience.)* Some people at this age are really not prepared to discuss all this, you know? It makes them feel just ... very ... humiliated.
MATTHEW. Have you?
KIM. No. I haven't.
MATTHEW. Has anyone ever performed oral sex on you?
KIM. Yes.
MATTHEW. And the circumstances — ?
KIM. A different boyfriend, also my junior year. We'd been at a party. We went back to my place about two or three in the morning. He was kissing me, and he started removing his clothes, and we were lying on the bed, and he ... he performed, you know, on me. And he tried to have intercourse, and I said no. He didn't have a condom, or any.... And then later he tried again, and you know ... I said no. And, and then, you know, he got dressed and —
MATTHEW. When you say that he tried to have sex, was he on top of you trying to insert himself?
KIM. He ... he placed a hand in my vagina and I panicked because I wasn't sure of, you know, what was going on. Then I realized it was his hand, and — he was aggressive, but like I said, nothing happened.
MATTHEW. When you say he performed on you, did he put his mouth on your vaginal area?
KIM. *(To audience.)* If anyone wants my definition of eternity, this would be it. I had to answer these kinds of questions repeatedly for the people from the CDC. They came to our house several times and asked me things like this on the living room couch. Later, when I filed my suit, I had to answer the same questions over again in a room filled with eight or

nine middle-aged men. Don't ever tell me I don't know what invasion of privacy is like.
MATTHEW.   Did you suffer any wounds or bleeding or soreness from this encounter?
KIM.   You mean *this* encounter, or the encounter with my boyfriend? *(To audience.)* Of course, the real embarrassment isn't even in the physical details they drag out of you. It's what becomes so obvious finally: that no matter how passionate I'd been about anyone in my life so far, it wasn't really passionate enough to ... try again after the door slammed. And then — for me, the door slammed for good.
LEE.
"I have a garden of my own
But so with roses overgrown,
And lilies, that you would it guess
To be a little wilderness."

KIM.   Are you going to read that whole poem?
LEE.   Just favorite parts. Honest. We're already on line 76.

"And all the springtime of the year
It — "

(To her.) The fawn, that is.
KIM.   I know.
LEE.
"It only loved to be there.
Among the beds of lilies, I
Have sought it oft, where it should lie;
Yet could not, till itself would rise,
Find it, although before mine eyes.
For, in the flaxen lilies' shade,
It like a bank of lilies laid.
Upon the roses it would feed,
Until its lips e'en seemed to bleed:
And then to me 'twould boldly trip,
And print thoses roses on my lip — "

KIM. This is a long section.
LEE. I'm almost done.
"But all its chief delight was still
On roses thus itself to fill:
And its pure virgin limbs to fold
In whitest sheets of lilies cold.
Had it lived long, it would have been
Lilies without, roses within."

KIM. Well, that's pretty.
LEE. I'm sorry you had to talk about those first experiences. There's a kind of loneliness that comes with first times. A longing. At least there was for me. You want it to go so easily, to glide, to be as effortless as that moment you first saw each other. You want your first time to be graceful as a smile. It's more like hand-to-hand combat. You struggle over every inch. This is all right, but that.... Up to here, but not.... You try to become completely lost in each other, and instead, you begin to understand what an elegant and effective prison the human body is.
KIM. When did you lose your virginity?
LEE. At twenty. *(Matthew laughs involuntarily.)* It could've been worse. Horatio Alger was nearly thirty when he lost his. The next day he wrote in his journal, "I was a fool to have waited so long."
KIM. *(To audience.)* My family got tested for HIV. My blood sister got tested. My old boyfriends got tested. None of them was positive. Questions got down to using my roommates' razors — roommates got tested, all negative. If I'd been able to say, "Yes, I had a transfusion once, or once I slept with a bisexual man who I think used drugs," the CDC would've said —
MATTHEW. Fine, thank you.
KIM. And that would've been it. That's all they do in the vast majority of cases: find a risk factor, and assume that's what it was. But I was a puzzle. I used to wonder if maybe I hadn't stepped on something on the beach. A syringe, or —
MATTHEW. And never noticed?
KIM. You don't know what to think. You've got this disease.

The best experts in the country can't tell you how. Meanwhile you're hiding it from as many people as possible, you're going through a kind of terror you've never known, you feel *guilty*. You feel as though you somehow betrayed your family, because you see their pain. And you yourself — somehow you betrayed yourself. You failed to take care of yourself. But how? How?

MATTHEW. *(Sitting U., smiling pleasantly.)* Hi.

KIM. Hi. *(They're strangers. Matthew pages through his "magazine.")* It took almost six months to get into a treatment program in Miami. I was in it with three men I didn't know. There was an actor, and a turnpike employee and a man who worked with autistic and retarded children. They were all gay.

MATTHEW. *(Friendly.)* Pretty quiet in here today.

KIM. Yeah.

MATTHEW. My name's Matthew. *(He looks at Lee.)*

KIM. Hi, I'm Kim.

MATTHEW. You on the program?

KIM. Yes.

MATTHEW. Me too. Just getting the basic package?

KIM. Guess so.

MATTHEW. I have black, hairy tongue.

KIM. Pardon?

MATTHEW. From all the medications. Black, hairy tongue — it's a reaction.

KIM. Oh.

MATTHEW. The taste buds. They swell and turn dark. Don't worry, I won't show you. Just don't get scared if you develop it, that's all. It's a side effect.

KIM. Oh. Thanks. *(He smiles at her; she smiles back. Matthew goes back to "reading." To audience.)* We were getting AZT and CD-4. I was already getting pentamidine. I got a prescription for Bactrim, to keep the pneumonia at bay. But at least I was on a program, and we all had hope at the time. I didn't develop black, hairy tongue, but suddenly everything tasted terrible. Plus there was a lot of nausea. They said I'd have to work through it and keep eating. I lost six pounds in one week. Gained one back, thank goodness.

MATTHEW. That's good.
KIM. Thanks. I shouldn't be complaining. I was chubby in college.
MATTHEW. Really?
KIM. I ended up losing it. But I was — I looked like a porker. Well, I thought I looked like a porker; my friends thought I looked normal, but that I just weighed a little too much. And I probably could've lost ten pounds.
MATTHEW. Who couldn't? Back then, anyway. My lover was overweight, a little bit. By the time he died, he was so thin, I couldn't believe I'd ever been with him. "That's not the body I made love to," I thought. "Who is this person?"
KIM. How's your weight?
MATTHEW. Oh — um ... better.
KIM. *(To audience.)* It was my mother who first thought of Dr. Acer. There'd been rumors about him. Some people thought he had AIDS. So we mentioned it to the CDC. What about the dentist? They said there's no chance I got it that way.
LEE. We're not investigating transmission from the dentist —
KIM. They said —
LEE. It's a dead end.
KIM. I was never told they were investigating the dentist. But of course, that's exactly what they were doing.
LEE. *(To audience.)* The Centers For Disease Control are required to be extremely secretive about the HIV cases they handle. I personally see the virtue of that. One of the few stigmas in this country more powerful than that which is attached to homosexuality, is the one attached to terminal illness. More powerful still is the stigma attached to contagious terminal illness. In Florida, they burned a family out of their home. In Poland, they stoned buildings that housed children with AIDS. In Egypt, a woman with AIDS had to have her baby delivered by her mother, since no doctors or nurses would do it. So about all the CDC can tell you is that they either do or don't know how you got infected, and ... thank you very much.
KIM. Seven months after I was diagnosed, Jane Pauley had

a message for me on the evening news. She said the CDC had released a report that a young woman in Florida my age had in all likelihood been infected with HIV by her dentist. No one had called to tell me this would be on.
LEE.   They couldn't.
KIM.   This was the first moment I realized they'd been lying to me all along — staring me in the eye, knowing I had a disease that was going to kill me, and refusing to tell me the truth.
LEE.   They did tell you the truth. This was how they told you.
KIM.   Then may the rest of the world be as frank with them.
MATTHEW.   *(To audience.)* There's an inflation that's not just economic. The price goes up on truth as well. Someone tells the truth that he's gay, and he's beaten to death. Someone admits he's HIV-positive, and his health insurance is cancelled.
LEE.   *(To audience.)* A decade into this epidemic, the price of truth is at an all-time high. I don't know much about market forces; I was debilitated long ago by a liberal arts education. But it seems to me that the price was driven up when the AIDS epidemic ran directly into the real epidemic. The one we don't even see as a disease.
KIM.   After the CDC announcement, my sister Allison said —
MATTHEW.   It's going to come out; they're going to find you.
KIM.   She said there'd be reporters all over the place. That what I really needed was a lawyer. Something — some kind of protection. But I didn't want anybody to know. They could've burned *my* house down. Finally I decided to do it. What if there were other people this had happened to? Was I really the only one in a country of 250 million? Were those the odds?
MATTHEW.   For every three million seeds created by the red alder, only one will grow into a new tree. *(Kim looks at Matthew, who looks at Lee.)* Why did I say that?
LEE.   Sorry. I looked up a lot of statistics — sort of in general.

MATTHEW. And I'm just supposed to toss them in?
LEE. They're counterpoint. You know ... to vary the presentation.
KIM. I thought it was going fine.
LEE. It was. I'm just drawn to statistics, that's all.
MATTHEW. What? You mean emotionally?
LEE. In a way. For example: *(To audience.)* A person would have to fly 30,000 times before they were due to crash in a plane.
MATTHEW. What's emotional about that?
LEE. Well ... the fear, I guess —
MATTHEW. So if I say far more people die at railroad crossings every year than in plane crashes, you have a specific, definable emotional response?
LEE. Yes.
MATTHEW. And you feel something — fear or pity or ... when I say that?
LEE. Yes.
MATTHEW. And if I say I have AIDS, and I'm dying? *(A beat.)* Do you feel something then? That you can ... hold onto? *(A beat.)* I'm just curious.
LEE. Of course ... of course. No, it's fine, just.... Let's go on for right now. *(A beat.)*
KIM. *(To audience.)* We went to a lawyer. It was a big office down in West Palm Beach. Bob Montgomery — my lawyer — thought we should seek damages, that there might be quite a bit, in fact. But there'd be a price — and he didn't mean his fee.
LEE. I mean your privacy.
KIM. We filed suit against Dr. Acer's insurance company and called a press conference. I met all of America pretty much at once. Everyone wanted to see the young woman who'd done the impossible: contracted HIV just sitting in a dentist's chair.
MATTHEW. The only one in the world. For a few months, you were the ultimate statistic.
KIM. *(To audience.)* The only one in the world. *That* got a few people interested. After awhile, it got hard for me to go

places without being recognized. *(She looks around to Matthew, who smiles.)*
MATTHEW. Hi.
KIM. Matthew — hi.
MATTHEW. I saw you on TV.
KIM. Oh, right.
MATTHEW. You looked very good.
KIM. Thanks.
MATTHEW. How's your treatment going?
KIM. My T-cells are at 43.
MATTHEW. Oh?
KIM. They don't think the CD-4's working. I'm going off it.
MATTHEW. I'm sorry.
KIM. They wanted to switch me over to a ddI/AZT combination —
MATTHEW. *(Nodding.)* Uh-hunh.
KIM. But you have to weigh 110 pounds, and I don't qualify. I'm down to 102.
MATTHEW. I'm sorry.
KIM. I may not qualify for anything down here in Miami anymore.
MATTHEW. What'll you do?
KIM. Switch back to the clinic at West Palm Beach. It's much closer to home.
MATTHEW. We'll miss you.
KIM. Thanks. *(After a beat, to Matthew.)* Yesterday, I called my friend with AIDS. Her husband has AIDS too, and their little boy's trying to deal with the fact that both his parents are sick.
MATTHEW. How's she doing?
KIM. Not very well. She has herpes sores at least two inches long all over the inside of her mouth. It makes it hard for her to eat. She had absolutely no white blood cells. It got down to zero. They had to give her a transfusion. *(A beat.)* I don't know why I'm thinking about her.
MATTHEW. I was going to walk over to Dunkin' Donuts. Want to come? *(She smiles.)*
LEE. *(To audience.)* The mass media went uniformly crazy

over Kim's story. They'd just had Alison Gertz on the cover of *People* two months before —
MATTHEW. You know — HIV from just one date? White girl? Upper East Side?
LEE. And they'd done Ryan White and the Ray family and well, they were more than ready for Kim.
KIM. I was ready for them, too. I had a few things to say. I was glad when all these people we'd only seen on TV knocked on our door and asked us to choose between them.
MATTHEW. Kim? You can't do both Donohue and Oprah.
KIM. Why not, Mom?
MATTHEW. *(To Lee.)* Why am I always her mother?
LEE. Please.
MATTHEW. Donohue's demanding an exclusive.
KIM. I'd rather do Oprah.
LEE. There's always Geraldo.
KIM. Dad — please.
LEE. How was your interview with Paula Zahn?
KIM. Better than the one with Deborah Norville.
MATTHEW. Oh, by the way — Larry King doesn't want to interview you unless you're willing to fly up. Plus he doesn't want your lawyer with you.
KIM. Everybody wants me to fly to them. I can't make that many trips. Maybe if I was eating well.
MATTHEW. It's your decision.
KIM. Let's hold out — ok?
LEE. Kim? The *National Enquirer* called again. They doubled their offer to $10,000.
KIM. Not interested.
LEE. They say they'll do the story whether they have you or not.
KIM. I'm not interested.
LEE. They say they'll print a story about the dentist being gay.
KIM. What's that got to do with it? I don't see how these people can live with themselves after they print this crap.
MATTHEW. Kim? Oprah says if you want to do her show, you have to come next week. She's going on vacation.

KIM. Ok. When's that film crew from the Netherlands?
LEE. Kim? *People* magazine said they'll fly your sister down from Gainesville on a private charter so she can be here for your interview.
KIM. *(To audience.)* It went on like this for a few months. Lasted a long time, I guess, as these things go. *Inside Edition* even sponsored a trip for me and my best friend Geralynn. I got to do some things I'd never done, and they got to have great ratings one night. We skiied in Utah, rode in a helicopter in the Grand Canyon and in a hot-air balloon in Palm Springs. That was the best. Geri and I just floating over these endless groves of palm trees in the desert. Floating again. For a few minutes, it seemed like a different planet. I started to imagine who might live down there. Maybe it was people who were not greedy, not vicious, not afraid. Maybe they felt pain when others suffered, joy when others succeeded. Impossible people, walking gracefully beneath the palms, approaching every new experience thoughtfully, generously — grateful just to be walking there at all. Then suddenly the balloon made a little jump, and I looked up and thought, "Here I am suspended above my dreams by nothing more than heat." It felt like riding in the hand of God — that gentle, that terrifying. And somehow I knew, that wherever that hand took me, frightened as I was, it would never let me go.
MATTHEW. I was going to go on a hot-air balloon. My friends arranged it for me. It was very windy that fall. We couldn't get a calm day. By the time the weather was good again, I couldn't walk.
LEE. Couldn't they have carried you?
MATTHEW. Wouldn't have mattered much by then. I'd gone just about blind.
KIM. In the middle of all the media attention, there was a pretty intense debate, of course. A lot of people didn't believe I was infected by Dr. Acer — no matter what the CDC said. But as more of Dr. Acer's patients turned up positive, it got harder to deny.
LEE. *(As a lawyer at a deposition.)* Doctor, where are you employed?

MATTHEW. *(As research scientist.)* Los Alamos National Laboratory.

LEE. And you were asked by the CDC to analyze the HIV nucleotide sequences as well as the amino acid sequences derived from the blood of this patient — referred to as Patient A — and the sequences derived from the blood of the dentist?

MATTHEW. That's right.

KIM. *(To audience.)* I was called Patient A a lot, since at first my name was off-limits. Then two of Dr. Acer's other patients tested positive, and we had Patients B and C. It felt insulting. As though they'd decided never to speak my name again.

MATTHEW. At least they studied your case. Most of us never get designated anything. Just the research equivalent of a mass grave.

LEE. Doctor, what did you find when you compared the sequences?

MATTHEW. Well for example, there are eight amino acids constituting the HIV signature. As it happens, there are some rare substitutions in the sequence signature of the dentist, and these substitutions are also found in Patients A, B, and C. However, they are not found in any of the Florida control group. So far, in fact, we haven't found this signature anywhere in our data base — except among this dentist and these three patients. It's a unique signature.

LEE. And what is the probability of that?

MATTHEW. The probability?

LEE. Yes, please.

MATTHEW. *(As himself.)* Are you sure about this study?

LEE. Believe me, this is the short form.

MATTHEW. *(As the scientist.)* Well, the probability would be 6.3 times the log base E, times to the minus seventh power.

LEE. And in English that would be — ?

MATTHEW. One in a million. Now as for the nucleotides —

KIM. *(To audience.)* I think the insurance company really thought about going to court until the other two patients were discovered. After that, the company agreed to a million-dollar settlement. They knew, as any judge reading the data would know, we got HIV the way we said.

LEE. *(A helpful, but odd person.)* Hello? I'm calling for Kimberly Bergalis. I too am a devout Catholic, though I live far away. I read in a national magazine about a clinic where a woman was cured of AIDS by exercise, natural diet and meditation. She only has scars now on her cells.

KIM. A lot of people wanted to cure me — especially after we won the settlement.

MATTHEW. *(A persisitent person.)* Hello, I've had a healing ability since 1987. I can cure the AIDS virus. AIDS is very similar to cancer, and if cancer can be stopped, so can AIDS. Remember, the newspapers don't print everything.

LEE. *(Another person.)* Hello, I'm sending a pamphlet about Urine Therapy.

MATTHEW. *(Overlapping, the persistent person.)* Hello, I'm calling for the third time. As a metaphysician, I have a healing ability. If you really want to save Kim's life, contact me at my New York office.

KIM. I'm sure it was with the best intentions.

MATTHEW. Those kinds of people called you?

KIM. All the time.

MATTHEW. Figures. I had to call them.

KIM. *(To audience.)* Others, from all over the country, sent books: "When Bad Things Happen To Good People," "God Calling." And they wrote really beautiful letters. A man fasted for 35 days in order to cure me. I was getting too sick to read much. It was easier to just lie there and watch the birds.

LEE. Kim's house takes getting used to. The living room's filled with five or six large birds with dangerous-looking beaks. They're not in cages — just around. And of course, they shriek a lot. *(Matthew shrieks like a parrot. He makes muted parrot sounds through the next two speeches only.)*

KIM. The birds show off for strangers. Didn't you like them?

LEE. No, no — I liked them fine. Birds have always fascinated me. It's just that the level of *life* in your house. All these creatures breathing and eating. Staring. I can barely take care of a cat. I'm always worried about what it's thinking. It

amazes me that people can draw all this life to them, that it somehow makes them more focussed, not less. The only birds I live with are in books.
MATTHEW. What books?
LEE. My favorite one's called *Extinct Birds.* The illustrations are quite —
MATTHEW. Pardon me — are we still on the point?
LEE. In a way. I think so. *(To audience.) Extinct Birds.* Um ... sometimes for relaxation I'll look through it. Not relaxation, really. It's more of an emotional experience. *(With a quick look at Matthew.)* It has what you'd expect: exquisite birds — all disappeared forever now. I knew all the stars: the Dodo, Passenger Pigeon, Great Auk. But sometimes I'll run across the most vivid picture of a bird I never knew existed — the Pink-Headed Duck, the Laughing Owl, the Paradise Parrot —
KIM. We had parrots.
LEE. Not this one. My favorite discovery was the Huia. That's "Hwee-Ah." New Zealand bird. Gone since ... 1907? For years naturalists thought that the male and female were two different species. They had completely different types of beaks, which has never been found in any other bird.
MATTHEW. I give this no hope at all of tying in.
LEE. The male broke up rotting wood with his short, thick beak, and the female would follow along extracting grubs with her longer, more delicate bill.
MATTHEW. And?
LEE. And therefore, when the bird was erased from existence, not only was it gone, but also its unique ... collaboration. That particular form of sharing is also dead.
MATTHEW. And all this gets us back to...?
LEE. I mean, we all discover that we're born into a world in which things have fallen away from us already. Irretrievably. Instances of life that — Forms of beauty. Things we never possessed, but somehow ... still feel we have the right to.
MATTHEW. You have the right to a bird from New Zealand?
LEE. No, to its uniqueness. *(To Kim.)* By the way, there is an irony.

KIM. Oh — lucky.
LEE. The Huia, a bird so beautiful it was hunted to extinction for its plumage, was named for its own distress call. *(A beat.)*
MATTHEW. That's it?
LEE. You see the connection, don't you?
MATTHEW. You want to know what I see? I'll tell you. I see a person who's deeply emotional.
LEE. You do?
MATTHEW. Yes. And the farther he gets from something that's human, the deeper emotion he feels. As it descends the Chain of Being from human, to animal, to dead animal, to the idea of a dead animal —
LEE. This isn't —
MATTHEW. I wish I was the last specimen of some bird of paradise. Some final display of worth that even you could understand. Something even you could miss — in your soul — when I was gone. *(A beat.)* Anyhow, that's what I see. Thanks for asking.
KIM. *(To audience.)* This was a relatively good time for me and my family. We were suddenly famous, we'd won this big settlement, and I was still having a lot of good days physically. Over the past year I'd been up to Pennsylvania to see relatives, old friends. Once I met a young man on the plane. He was, well, good-looking. And I still looked ok, and ... I could tell he was attracted to me. He didn't know who I was. I admit I sort of gave in to the fantasy for a little while — you know, of kind of flirting in a real sweet way. Not telling him. *(She looks at Matthew, smiles.)* Hi.
MATTHEW. *(Turning to Lee.)* Oh, no. No, no. No way.
LEE. *(To Kim.)* Sorry.
KIM. It's ok. It was just a couple hours anyway. Then the plane landed. *(A beat.)* Not long after that, our priest started to call. Father Chris. We'd known him forever.
LEE. Kim —
KIM. He said —
LEE. There's someone I'd like you to see. He's about your age.

KIM. About my age and dying of cancer. But I went to see him. He wasn't doing that great. They gave him morphine shots while I was there. When I left, I cried and cried. I went three or four times that week. The next week, the boy died. Anyway, Father Chris made his point — at least what I took to be his point. I thought, "I have AIDS. But I can walk and see and feel and touch. I can run and bend." And of course there was another point that took me longer to understand. Father Chris was reminding me that in all likelihood, and sooner rather than later, I would be like this boy. When you're 22, it's hard to know what that is, unless you go and look at it.

LEE. *(To audience, as her priest.)* No one wants to see the priest coming. People see me on my way, dressed in black — they know what it's about. Mortality is my job. Plenty reject what I do, and that's their right. But for those who believe —

MATTHEW. I'm lapsed.

LEE. For those who believe — eventually they don't see death coming, dressed all in black. They see life.

KIM. *(To audience.)* Anyway, I was grateful. I had a church that supported me, I had my family, the community, I had money — I knew how many people with AIDS didn't have any of that. My Mom worked in a clinic. I knew what those people went through.

MATTHEW. Then why did you inflict more pain on them?

(Kim looks at Matthew, then at Lee.)

KIM. Is that why he's here?

LEE. Sort of. One reason.

KIM. Thanks a lot.

LEE. I have to be responsible.

KIM. *(To audience.)* I called a few people bastards before I died, and frankly I don't regret it. I resented what that dentist did, but more than that I resented the authorities who told him he had a right to keep practicing and keep his secret. After all, when you die for a public health policy, I think you have the right to question it pretty strenuously. And this principle doesn't just apply to me. AIDS activists, who themselves die every day for any number of public health policies,

aren't the least bit shy about making their views known. And like myself, they take advantage of whatever public forum is offered.
MATTHEW. But you had a broader forum. And you were speaking for so many fewer people.
KIM. *(To Lee.)* Is he going to be this way from now on?
LEE. It's the chance you take. You put a character onstage —
KIM. *(Irritably.)* Oh, *right!* *(To Matthew.)* This may seem like a very selfish point of view, but I considered my life to be more important than a debatable public health policy. Four more people will probably die because of what Dr. Acer was allowed to do. Exactly how many lives should a public health policy be worth?
MATTHEW. You want an honest answer?
KIM. Yes!
LEE. *(To audience, as he intervenes between the two.)* Actually, the answer is quite variable depending on who's in the White House, how much money's to be made and what kind of field-day Congress and/or the media are having. But public health policies have in the past gone for a price of — easily — hundreds of thousands of lives. That's why to many it seems so ... paltry to talk about the six lives in this case. After all, it's been a couple years. Other physicians have succumbed to AIDS, and so far none of their patients was shown to be infected.
MATTHEW. Which is the whole point.
LEE. Is it? I mean, we're doing studies and we think we're right when we say we don't see any further cases. But people with a risk factor are just charged off to that risk factor. Some of them, for all we know — and I'm certainly not talking about many — might have been infected by a health care worker instead. And we just never noticed.
MATTHEW. Do you really believe that?
LEE. I don't know. But do you really believe that no health care worker will ever infect a patient with HIV again?
MATTHEW. Not if they follow universal precautions.
LEE. If. People die for if. She died for if. I don't know

what to think about a phrase like "universal precautions." I mean, haven't we all seen enough episodes of *Emergency?* The blood goes flying — before people can get gloves on. Doctors try to stick hypos into men who've been shot in the gut, flopping around like fish. People get stuck. How confident do I feel when I hear a phrase like "universal precautions?" They're not universal. They're only as universal as we can make them. And is that good enough?

MATTHEW. Absolutely.

KIM. Never.

MATTHEW. Public health policy has to be made for 250 million people. Not six, or a hundred or ten thousand — 250 million. The only solution to this epidemic lies in the work of the medical community. We can't turn them into a persecuted class.

LEE. So someone dies? Or may die?

MATTHEW. Someone dies every day, of something! You spend all this time and effort over the lives of a few people —

KIM. Whether it's a few —

MATTHEW. A *few! (To Kim.)* You knew some people who died of AIDS-related causes? I knew hundreds. I spent years watching my acquaintances, my friends, my lovers — the one true family of my world, *my world* — die one by one. And no one in the rest of this country gave a damn. They were happy in fact — either that homosexuals were dying *per se,* or that the disease seemed thankfully to be confined to a single, disenfranchised group. Then I got to watch as the rest of America discovered HIV case by heterosexual case — from Ryan White, to Alison Gertz, to you, to Magic Johnson to Arthur Ashe. I got to watch tributes to the courage of these brave, suffering human beings. Outpourings of affection from people they would never meet, whose thoughts were with them every day, whose eyes filled with tears that these lives could be cut short, that these lives — which were so precious that no amount of publicity was too much — had been mutilated by a virus that was clearly meant for someone else. Then I got to die. In oblivion. Because no matter how many thousands of us die, we will never be visible to you.

LEE. *(To audience.)* It's hard to write about a mass of people. Far easier to focus on an individual. I like to think — I hope it's true — that it's hard for me to dismiss any life. But I suppose I do. And not just out of fear or misunderstanding. *(A beat.)* My brother died when he was twenty. Many years ago. One-car accident. It was an old car, no seat belts. The kind of seat belts that would have saved his life were still years away, though the technology had been there for decades. We as a society were sacrificing maybe 10,000 people a year this way. It really wasn't a big enough number to make us change our public policy. He's been dead for over 25 years. And each year, on April 16th, though I don't plan to, I notice that it's his birthday again. Someone dies every day, of something. *(A beat.)*
"Oh, help! Oh, help! I see it faint:
And die as calmly as a saint.
See how it weeps. The tears do come
Sad, slowly dropping like a gum.
So weeps the wounded balsam: so
The holy frankincense doth flow.
The brotherless Heliades — "

(To Kim.) The Heliades were the sisters of —
KIM. It's all right.
LEE. They were turned into poplar trees. And their tears into amber.

"The brotherless Heliades
Melt in such amber tears as these."

KIM. Not that long after my trip out west, floating in the balloon, I took a turn for the worse. Hospital, transfusion — that's when Lee met me. My lawyer had given him a really nice picture they'd taken of me the fall before, and I was glad, because I was beginning to look a lot worse. When I left the hospital this time, I started keeping my diary on tape, 'cause I was too weak to write. I'd lie on the couch all day, making tapes. You can hear our parrots on parts of them. Sometimes, I'd talk to my sisters. Allison held up really well, but Sondra cried a lot. She was only eleven. I was kind of another mom to her, and I knew it wasn't good for her to lose somebody right then. Anyway, she'd start crying and just couldn't stop sometimes, and I'd have to think of things to cheer her up. Like once I said, "Listen — every time there's a graduation, or if you give a big speech, I want you to save a seat for me. If you get married, I want there to be a seat. And you know what? I guarantee you, you'll feel a presence. You're going to be happy, and you're going to smile, and you're going to say, 'Kim's here.' Ok? Now, I want that seat. You've got to promise me. If you have a child, I want a seat when you have that child. It might make me sick, but I want to see that first child born. Ok, now I'm getting too mooshy and enough has been said, but is everybody ok? Does everyone feel a little better?" 'Course, by that time we were *all* crying. *(A beat.)* Not long after that, speaking became harder. I was weak and my voice had turned into this monotonic whine wrapped around what was becoming a kind of constant pain. By the end of May, I couldn't speak at all. I was at home, and I had a nurse, but we weren't doing much medically. Just treating symptoms. I was on the couch all summer, silent.

MATTHEW. You weren't so silent in September. *(Indicating the audience.)* May I? *(She nods.)* Kimberly, as America loved to call her, was by her own definition, an "innocent" person with AIDS. And she was right, of course, since who isn't? But she was more than just innocent in the public mind. She was a virgin who'd been outraged — everybody's daughter, the dream of the republic. And while she'd never have a chance to have a go at the Virgin birth, she was at least guaranteed the Virgin death.

KIM. Are you saying I wasn't a virgin? Because the insurance companies made me take two full physicals. They drew pictures of my hymen.

MATTHEW. No, I'm not denying you were a virgin. Or as close as we get to it anymore.

KIM. Thank you.

MATTHEW. It really doesn't matter what you were. The only thing that mattered was what politicians could make of you.
LEE. *(To audience.)* Which was, as one commentator put it, "the Willie Horton of AIDS."
MATTHEW. Exactly. And mandatory testing laws were drafted. Disclosure laws. You proved a great opportunity for a number of powerful people who hate homosexuals: Pat Buchanan, William Dannemeyer, Jesse Helms — it was a very admirable crew.
KIM. They agreed with my position.
MATTHEW. And that didn't scare you?
LEE. It scared me. Still does.
KIM. I wasn't fighting homosexuals. I wasn't fighting people who had AIDS, or doctors or ... I just don't think any doctor should go into my body if he has HIV and hasn't told me. I didn't care what sort of politicians agreed with that, or why they agreed.
MATTHEW. Sort of a one-issue person?
KIM. Yes, I sort of was.
MATTHEW. *(To audience.)* Anyhow, this wonderful law they'd drafted — called the Kimberly Bergalis Patient and Health Providers' Protection Act — was going to be voted on in the fall, so in September they had hearings. Kimberly was invited to be a witness.
KIM. My voice came back — it didn't sound any better, but it came back — in August. I wasn't able to walk much by the time of the hearings. We took the train up.
MATTHEW. Her parents accompanied her. By now, the ugly political reality was this: the new law being debated was a dead letter. It was more than a year since Dr. Acer's case had been uncovered, and surveys had found no other health care worker in the country having infected a patient with HIV. Public furor was beginning to ebb. The Bergalises may well have guessed this, but came anyway because it would at least provide a public forum — something that was getting harder for them to find. Kim's comments to the committee were brief and didn't offer anything new in the debate —

KIM. *(Cutting him off with her comments to the committee.)* "I'd like to say that AIDS is a terrible disease that we must take seriously. I did nothing wrong, yet I'm being made to suffer like this. My life has been taken away. Please enact legislation so that no other patient or health care provider will have to go through the hell that I have. Thank you." *(To Matthew.)* For the record.

MATTHEW. *(To audience.)* Her father also spoke, and seemed to suggest that if these congressmen didn't pass this law they were probably all damned to hell. Which, considering what they did for a living, may have been a foregone conclusion. In any case, the Kimberly Bergalis Act was supported only by the committee's right-wing Republicans, and never even came up for a vote. Kimberly's speech —

KIM. Was the last public act of my life.

LEE. After testifying, the family went to the White House. A tour had earlier been arranged. There had been some mixed signals as to whether President Bush and his wife — who were home at the time — would be greeting them personally. The Bergalises didn't know who they'd be meeting from the Administration. The answer was, in its way, sublime.

KIM. Nobody.

MATTHEW. The President's personal quarters are on the second floor. He doesn't have to come down. Oh, he would be down later — there was a dinner that evening for the King of Morocco.

KIM. We saw the place-settings.

MATTHEW. In the end, they were shown around by a reluctant Secret Service agent.

LEE. Kim's mother told me she had an almost irresistible urge to shout up the stairs.

MATTHEW. *(As Kim's mother.)* George?! Babs?! We're here! Come on down! *(A beat.)* George?!

LEE. George?!

MATTHEW. Millie?!

KIM. My family wheeled me out of the White House, and we all went home to Florida.

MATTHEW. We hope you've enjoyed your tour of the

American political process.
KIM.   After the trip to Washington, as far as most of America was concerned, I was pretty much used up. Too sick for talk shows, Congress wasn't going to pass my law, the President had missed his photo opportunity. Time to go back to the couch and count the parrots and ... pass away.
MATTHEW.   Pass away. A phrase obviously not invented for AIDS.
KIM.   I lived two and a half more months. It's easier to die in public life than in real life.
MATTHEW.   I wouldn't know. You're right about real life, though. What was my list? Pneumonia, blindness, dementia finally — for which I was grateful, since it allowed me to forget about the enormous debt, and the fact that almost everyone I knew had gone out of my life before I did.
KIM.   You were alone?
MATTHEW.   Oh, no. There were medical personnel.
KIM.   I wanted to die at home. Not every family can bear that. I mean, you've been so disfigured. You wonder who they're looking at when they talk to you — if maybe afterwards they don't go into the bedroom and look at your old high-school picture.
MATTHEW.   I hated my high-school picture.
KIM.   Me too. *(Quietly.)* I don't want to talk about when I died.
LEE.   *(To audience.)* Anna and George told me that Kim had good nights and bad nights. Of course the good nights now resembled the bad nights of a few months before. Kim hadn't yet experienced the final effects of the disease. Incontinency, incoherence. The intense pain. But these were coming, they knew. One day in December, Kim suddenly thanked her nurse for having taken such good care of her. That night, getting her ready for bed, Anna and George said to their daughter — and this is something I can only imagine since I've never fathered children of my own —
KIM.   You can let go, Kim.
MATTHEW.   It's ok.
KIM.   You don't have to worry about us.

MATTHEW. You don't have to go through the pain.
KIM. You can just let go.
LEE. That night Anna decided to sleep on the floor of Kim's room, next to her bed. Sometime later the dog came in, and laid down on the floor beside her. One of the things I admire about the Bergalises is how unassumingly they accept the work of living. And dying. All those months they kept Kim part of their family, part of their household. Each day she was on that couch in the middle of the living room. They didn't want to be apart from her. Each night they bathed her and put her to bed. It was clear she was going to die soon. The only question was, in how much pain? That night, very late, in the dark, Anna woke to a kind of scratching sound, a rattling. It was the dog. He was shuddering in his sleep and his claws were rattling against the door. Then Anna noticed Kim's breathing had stopped. Anna felt her. There was no pulse. Her body was still warm. Anna stood there for a moment, holding Kim's hand and the oddest emotion welled up in her, and she said to Kim —
MATTHEW. I'm so happy for you.
LEE. And she stood there in the ineffable excitement of the dark, feeling something beautiful had happened. Like a child on Christmas eve, suddenly certain that the house had been visited, and the long dreamed-of gift had at last been given.
KIM. Mom waited for a while, then went and woke my Dad and told him. They sat there for a long time, in the stillness that's already come to so many parents, and will come to so many more.
MATTHEW. Someone held my hand when I died. I think it was the day nurse. She had a peculiar smell.
LEE.
"Now my sweet fawn is vanished to
Whither the swans and turtles go:
In fair Elysium to endure,
With milk-white lambs, and ermines pure.
Oh, do not run too fast: for I
Will but bespeak thy grave, and die."
(To audience.) The Nymph — the young girl, the speaker of

the poem — is planning her own death, because she can't survive in a world that has murdered innocence.
MATTHEW. Sounds like a quitter.
LEE. I suppose. *(To audience.)* But I sympathize with her. You know, one recent estimate I saw suggests that at present rates, as many as a billion human beings — nearly one out of every six people in the world — could be HIV-infected as of the first couple decades in the next century.
MATTHEW. Don't do any more statistics.
LEE. Why not?
MATTHEW. I want you to describe something.
LEE. What?
MATTHEW. My funeral.
LEE. *(Uncomfortable.)* Your...?
MATTHEW. When I died. Did they bury me? Cremate? What?
LEE. What did you direct?
MATTHEW. I kept putting it off. By the time I started planning, I was too sick to — Was I buried?
LEE. It was cold. The ground was — A tough time to bury, anyway. You were cremated.
MATTHEW. Ah.
LEE. One relative. A cousin. Actually, she married into the family.
MATTHEW. *(Nodding.)* Mm-hmm.
LEE. She didn't know you very well, but ... she's a natural at tying up loose ends. She flew in quietly, accepted your ashes, knew she couldn't bring them home, so ... she thought about where to scatter them.
MATTHEW. Which was?
LEE. Where do you think?
MATTHEW. The park?
LEE. She waited for a warm day. She even asked where they plant the roses in the summer. And there, at noon, under a brilliant March sun —
MATTHEW. Oh.
LEE. There were a lot of ashes. The box was heavy. It felt

like a gallon of milk. So it took a long time. And a lot of rosebeds.
MATTHEW. And then she flew home?
LEE. Without looking back.
MATTHEW. Well ... I suppose that's all you need.
LEE. I suppose. *(To audience.)* It'll take a lot of effort to achieve one billion infected people. But we may have what it takes. Sometimes what concerns me most is that a cure will be found — for HIV, for all the deadly viruses we've begun to encounter. I suppose we'll declare victory again, ignoring as always the larger disease: the cowardice, the viciousness with which we behaved. It's the epidemic that's been with us from the beginning. Palpable everywhere, instantly recognizable, but with no simple acronym.
KIM. So you think that if we find the cure for AIDS tomorrow, we'll still have failed? *(A beat.)* How does the poem end?
LEE. The poem? It's nothing much. Just sort of an extended image. The girl, still in tears, imagines her own gravesite. You know, complete with a statue, and —
KIM. Let me hear.
LEE. Really? *(She nods.)*

"First my unhappy statue shall
Be cut in marble; and withal,
Let it be weeping too — but there
The engraver sure his art may spare,
For I so truly thee bemoan,
That I shall weep though I be stone:
Until my tears, still dropping, wear
My breast, themselves engraving there."

You understand? The statue will weep and —
KIM. *(Nodding.)* Keep going.
LEE.
"There at my feet shalt thou — "
KIM. The fawn.
LEE. Yes.

"There at my feet shalt thou be laid,
Of purest alabaster made:
For I would have thine image be
White as I can, though not as thee."

KIM. That's the end?
LEE. Yes.
KIM. I'm not going to have a statue.
LEE. I know.
KIM. But I was innocent.
LEE. The world is innocent. You know why?
KIM. Why?
LEE. Because the opposite of innocence is not guilt. It's knowledge.
KIM. And we're in the dark?
LEE. Completely.
KIM. How do you know?
LEE. Because I have no faith.
KIM. No faith at all? *(Lee shakes his head no.)* Then we're different. *(Lights slowly narrow in on Kim during the next speech.)* Eight months before I died, I was in pretty bad shape for a while. And I wanted to be prepared if something happened, so I was making all these plans and I realized maybe I should have the final blessing — the Sacrament of the Sick — so I made a phone call to a priest. Not Father Chris; he was out of town. This was around nine in the evening. And this priest said he'd come over right away. I said, I don't need it right now, but eventually I'd like to have this done. And he said, "No, no, no — I'm coming right over," and he hung up. So suddenly I'm trying explain to my parents why there's a priest coming to our house at 9 o'clock at night. They think I'm telling them that I'm dying tonight. And it's just this big mess. Everybody's crying. "What are you saying to us?" And I say, "No, I'm not dying tonight. I just need to talk to him and have this little blessing." And they didn't believe me. "Why are you having this done, Kim? Do you know something you're not telling us? Did you get some kind of calling?" I said *no*. I started crying and said the main reason I wanted him here

was that I was afraid to go to sleep, because I was afraid I wouldn't wake up. And that's one of the main reasons I hadn't been sleeping lately. Anyway, the priest came over, and we sat down in my room and he said some prayers, and I told him about a vision I thought I had a week before. I was in the dark and saw this dim light that moved around and went farther and farther away. And it turned into a bunch of little children, and they were waving at me and laughing. And it sounded like they were saying, "Come play, come play." Actually, I wasn't sure if they were saying, "Come play" or "Goodbye," but it sounded more like, "Come play." And then they disappeared. And the priest said that sometimes it's not always a vision — sometimes it's just a hallucination because I have a fever of 103 or 104. He said maybe it scared me, that they were calling me, and made me think it was my time. He said, "When the Lord is ready, He'll be ready. Don't necessarily think it's over yet." And my Mom brought up a good point. She said, "Why are you so sure that it's not going to get any worse? That it's going to be a quiet death, and not some more terrible thing? You may have more things happen to you." And that's something I never thought about. I just thought how *I* can't take this pain anymore, and how *I* feel about this pain, and how *I* want to be out of my misery before it gets worse. But God might not take me now. So that made me think. Well, anyway, the priest was really nice, and he gave me the Sacrament of the Sick, which I discovered I'd been getting all along at church, at weekly Mass. It's the exact same thing. And he gave me First Holy Communion, and then he left and I just felt so good suddenly. I started thinking again about the cemetary where I was going to be buried, and all the names —

MATTHEW. *(Quietly, in the background, as she continues.)* Zebleckas —

KIM. And how I'm going to lie right next to my grandmother on top of that mountain —

LEE. Pilashusky —

KIM. And how I'm going to lift up and just fly away into the heavens —

MATTHEW. Shucavage —
KIM. And how God's going to come down and take my hand —
LEE. Andrukitis —
KIM. And how my body's just going to be this thing I used while I was on this Earth.
MATTHEW. Karalunas —
KIM. Anyway, then this peace came over me, and I was able to sleep.
LEE. Bergalis. *(Lights fade to black.)*

THE END

NEW PLAYS

★ **RABBIT HOLE by David Lindsay-Abaire.** Winner of the 2007 Pulitzer Prize. Becca and Howie Corbett have everything a couple could want until a life-shattering accident turns their world upside down. "An intensely emotional examination of grief, laced with wit." *–Variety.* "A transcendent and deeply affecting new play." *–Entertainment Weekly.* "Painstakingly beautiful." *–BackStage.* [2M, 3W] ISBN: 978-0-8222-2154-8

★ **DOUBT, A Parable by John Patrick Shanley.** Winner of the 2005 Pulitzer Prize and Tony Award. Sister Aloysius, a Bronx school principal, takes matters into her own hands when she suspects the young Father Flynn of improper relations with one of the male students. "All the elements come invigoratingly together like clockwork." *–Variety.* "Passionate, exquisite, important, engrossing." *–NY Newsday.* [1M, 3W] ISBN: 978-0-8222-2219-4

★ **THE PILLOWMAN by Martin McDonagh.** In an unnamed totalitarian state, an author of horrific children's stories discovers that someone has been making his stories come true. "A blindingly bright black comedy." *–NY Times.* "McDonagh's least forgiving, bravest play." *–Variety.* "Thoroughly startling and genuinely intimidating." *–Chicago Tribune.* [4M, 5 bit parts (2M, 1W, 1 boy, 1 girl)] ISBN: 978-0-8222-2100-5

★ **GREY GARDENS book by Doug Wright, music by Scott Frankel, lyrics by Michael Korie.** The hilarious and heartbreaking story of Big Edie and Little Edie Bouvier Beale, the eccentric aunt and cousin of Jacqueline Kennedy Onassis, once bright names on the social register who became East Hampton's most notorious recluses. "An experience no passionate theatergoer should miss." *–NY Times.* "A unique and unmissable musical." *–Rolling Stone.* [4M, 3W, 2 girls] ISBN: 978-0-8222-2181-4

★ **THE LITTLE DOG LAUGHED by Douglas Carter Beane.** Mitchell Green could make it big as the hot new leading man in Hollywood if Diane, his agent, could just keep him in the closet. "Devastatingly funny." *–NY Times.* "An out-and-out delight." *–NY Daily News.* "Full of wit and wisdom." *–NY Post.* [2M, 2W] ISBN: 978-0-8222-2226-2

★ **SHINING CITY by Conor McPherson.** A guilt-ridden man reaches out to a therapist after seeing the ghost of his recently deceased wife. "Haunting, inspired and glorious." *–NY Times.* "Simply breathtaking and astonishing." *–Time Out.* "A thoughtful, artful, absorbing new drama." *–Star-Ledger.* [3M, 1W] ISBN: 978-0-8222-2187-6

DRAMATISTS PLAY SERVICE, INC.
440 Park Avenue South, New York, NY 10016 212-683-8960 Fax 212-213-1539
postmaster@dramatists.com www.dramatists.com